The House of Yearning

The House of Yearning

Poems by

Nina Bennett

Kelsay Books

Cover art: Kristyn Hodgdon
Cover design: Shay Culligan

ISBN: 13-978-1-947465-41-1

Kelsay Books
Aldrich Press
www.kelsaybooks.com

*In memory of
my sister Blair, my granddaughter Madeline,
and my father, Jim Bennett*

Love is eternal

Acknowledgments

Grateful acknowledgment to the following publications where these poems first appeared, sometimes in slightly different versions

Big River Poetry Review: "How to Get to the House of Yearning"
Drash: Northwest Mosaic: "Demeter's Garden"
Hamilton Stone Review: "Semper Fi"
Hartskill Review: "The Before Time"
Main Street Journal: "After Care," "Traveling Companions"
Philadelphia Stories: "Love, Vincent"
Poetry Breakfast: "Resurrection"
Red River Review: "Dia de Muertos"
The Broadkill Review: "My Sister's Bracelet," "Diamonds on the Soles of Her Shoes," "Mind The Gap," "Mt. Tibidabo,"
The Healing Muse: "A phone call after midnight"
Victorian Violet: "Sand-Written"
Wilderness House Literary Review: "Waldo Canyon Wildfire"

"Symphony in E Minor" included in *Joy Interrupted-an anthology on motherhood and loss,* ed. Melissa Miles McCarter

Contents

Roots

Ninety-five degrees, and I'm on my knees
prying weeds from the cracked concrete
driveway in front of my childhood home.

My father constructed an igloo
on the right side of our driveway
one February. Packed cardboard
shoeboxes with snow, played
the hose over the dome until it froze.

I practiced coming to a stop,
wobbled down the drive on roller skates
tightened to shoes with a key. Dad
stood in the street, arms
extended like a scarecrow.

On the far left, a faint stain from the load
of manure Dad once ordered as a Mother's Day gift.
Noses wrinkled from the stench,
my sister and I watched our father
fill the wheelbarrow, push it to Mum's rose garden.

Behind me, the mismatched panel
on the garage door, busted
when my sister steered our mother's car
too close as she tried to sneak out
before she got her driver's license.

Now all of them dead but me, crumbled
specks of concrete pressed into my skin
as I use a rusty screwdriver to loosen roots.

I Never Told

though it pissed me off when you borrowed
my clothes, left them dirty, crumpled
on your closet floor. Never said
where I was going, lied so you wouldn't
tag along. It was me who told Dad
you smoked. Not the pot,
just the Marlboros.

You and Lizzie took Mom's car,
sneaked the spare key from her jewelry
box, cut school, drove to the beach.
I vacuumed sand for hours, screamed
at you until you slammed the bedroom door
on my hand, leaving a curved

scar on my ring finger. I had a
sloshed husband, two sons, no
money to attend your college
graduation. I never told you
I was proud, never ended
a phone call, love you sis.

Mom described your bulletin board
plastered with pictures of my boys,
brought back a box with my high
school yearbook, Doors albums
lifted from my room, that fringed
suede vest I sewed in 1968.

At the bottom, every letter
I ever sent you, creased
and worn, last one still crisp,
unopened. Mom found it in your mailbox,
delivered three days after you died.

Diamonds on the Soles of Her Shoes

for BAB

Fourth of July, 1987.
Oh say can you see
We donated her corneas,
the only organs undamaged.
A man in Wisconsin saw
his toddler granddaughter
for the first time.

Nobody raced
to pick up the phone
when it rang Saturday,
by the dawn's early light.
Outside the window mist hovered,
her father paced the lawn, pleaded
with the rising sun.

The house wrapped its walls
around her friends as they gathered,
told stories, listened to Paul Simon,
Steve Winwood, the music played
in her hospital room.
What so proudly we hailed at the twilight's last gleaming
.

Showers of red, white and blue
streaked the night,
bombs bursting in air,
an impromptu wake.

O'er the land of the free
Released from pain,
from tubes and machines,
the week-long vigil
in the trauma center.

We say farewell,
entrust her to *the rocket's red glare,*
the moon, the stars
and the home of the brave.

My Sister's Bracelet

When the box arrives
I place it unopened
in my top dresser drawer,
where it sits for several days.
Late at night, alone
in the room that used to be hers,
I slowly peel away the heavy
brown paper, thinking
there should be a ritual
for this sort of thing.
Squeezed snugly on my thin wrist,
the silver cuff outlasts
two wedding bands and the grubby
hands of three grandchildren.

After Care

We held my sister's wake in the townie
bar of the Deer Park tavern, my brother
and I drinking as though we were still
in college. Later there was a band,
and the singer's familiar voice
startled me sober. In high school

I did my homework during band practice,
sprawled on the basement floor
of the bass player's house. Forty years
later you tell me you spent band
practice staring at my ass as I lay on
my stomach studying. I don't tell you
that your voice still haunts my nights.

How to Get to The House of Yearning

Start at a bend in the road, a blind
curve running along the river.
Hear water race over rocks,
feel the chill as it plunges down
the mountain.

Find the home she abandoned
when she left her husband
because he didn't want children.
He lives there now with his second wife
and step-daughter.

Drive past the place she rented
on I street. Picture skis and snow shoes
on the front porch, next to the mountain
bike she rode to work.

Make your way to the trauma center
where she died on the Fourth of July,
Paul Simon's Graceland
the sound-track of her dying.

Fly across the country to a college town.
Head west, past the country club
where Jews weren't welcome.
Turn left at the field stone sign.
Pull into the driveway graced
by a weeping willow, join
her parents for a glass of wine.
You have arrived.

Demeter's Garden

The year my sister died, our mother
tilled her flower beds with bare hands.
From my bedroom window I watched

her shoulders shake as she labored
in the soil at dawn, exhumed dormant daylilies
with fingernails grown ragged. Bent over,

she rocked methodically the way an Orthodox Jew
davens during prayer, shaped precise rows
of shallow holes, positioned bulbs

the size of embryos, smoothed and patted
topsoil with the same tenderness
she once settled covers over us.

The following May, she pinched off slender
blue buds of wood hyacinths
paling towards their fragile tips.

Mind the Gap

Built-in shelves flank the fireplace,
hold dozens of family photos.
Royal Gorge, Colorado.
My parents stand next to a plaque, blue
and gold letters spell our state name.
My younger brother and I, opposite
our parents, connected from
shoulder to hip, fill the space
where the middle child should be.

My grandchildren together
in a posed portrait. The oldest
stretched on his side like a cat
in the summer sun. His sister
leans back against his legs,
her arms support their cousin
who at four months can't quite
sit on her own. Though
carefully arranged, the picture
is unable to conceal the gap
where the baby's big sister belongs.

Symphony in E Minor

Overture

The months of my daughter-in-law's
first pregnancy pass more quickly
for me than her. An early ultrasound
doesn't determine gender.
Midwife thinks girl,
urine DNA test purchased
online pronounces boy. My preference
isn't one of gender; secretly I hope
for a redheaded grandchild.

First Movement

The baby dances to Dave Matthews,
keeps the beat when my son talks.
For Father's Day I crawl through the attic,
find his bent hardback copies
of *Goodnight Moon* and
Where The Wild Things Are,
purchase fleece coveralls
that look like lime sherbet,
a gender-neutral color ideally suited
to red hair. My grocery cart
is taken over by disposable diapers
and tubes of Boudreaux's Butt Paste,
bought because I like the name.

Second Movement

A CD plays softly in the yellow
birthing suite, where windows
on two walls let in the fading light
of mid-November. Labor
progresses like an orchestra tuning,
cacophony of squeals and screeches.
Unable to find her note, she seeks
the comfort of the tub.

Third Movement

She pants and blows, cheeks
puffed out in exaggerated
mimicry of the woodwind section.
Gradually the head emerges,
turns awkwardly to permit
passage of first one shoulder,
then the other,
quickly followed by the realization
the baby isn't breathing. The cadence of CPR
fills the room like a metronome-
one and two and three and still
her heart doesn't beat.

Fourth Movement

I cradle my granddaughter
warm from the womb,
kiss her red eyebrows.
My son brings his baby home
in a porcelain urn
painted with dragonflies

instead of the dark blue
safety rated car seat.
I set aside my classic rock
and listen to Mahler's Kindertotenlieder.

The Before Time

after "Child," by Wendy Brown-Baez

In the before time, before he learned
babies die, my son grinned with ease,
mouth curved upward as his beam
claimed his hazel eyes. He sang
in the shower, whistled as he sprinted
down the driveway to fetch the mail.

He decorated the nursery,
hung a dreamcatcher over the crib,
placed his grandfather's kaleidoscope
on a shelf by the window.

My son's hands felt his daughter dance
in the womb in the before time, before
they held a ceramic urn the size of a coffee mug.

Now his hands are stilled, his belly laugh
no longer roars like a runaway train. Yesterday
his wife found him on his knees by the mailbox,
collapsed under the weight of a magazine
with a red-headed baby on the cover.

I twirl the kaleidoscope, search
for my son's smile. Multi-colored
glass chips tumble into place. Magenta,
fuchsia, violet, colors of a bruise.

Dia de Muertos

I coax marigolds from seed, place them on the hearth
beneath the picture of my infant granddaughter.
A sugar skull rests in front of the photograph. Her name,
Maddy, etched in fuschia icing. Bowls of nuts and fruits
on either side, anything to beckon *los angelitos*.
My *ofrenda* has a cocoa-colored teddy bear,
folded receiving blanket, two dragonfly fetishes.
Sandalwood incense permeates the living room,
reminds me of my teenage bedroom. I light a lamp
so my granddaughter can find her way when the gates
of heaven open at midnight. The dim glow casts a shadow
along the hallway, like the trail of pixie dust that follows
Tinkerbell.

Sand-Written

Her name, Maddy, etched on a North Shore
beach, bold strokes drawn in the wet sand.
Sweep of the right tail on the M reaches
for the shy curve of the y.
First and last letters cup the middle three,
hands cradling a newborn, holding her up
as an offering to the Hawaiian gods.

Ocean foam slides across the sand,
teases the top of the M, retreats.
A hefty wave breaks close to shore,
rushes in, pushes water over the letters,
pulls them out as it recedes in slow motion.
Sea glass glistens, a sand crab
scrambles to safety, and I lose her
yet again.

Symmetry No. 45

after M.C. Escher, 1941

If you stare at an Escher print
secondary images emerge.
They sharpen, blur, sharpen again
in the flicker of the candle's flame.
Bats turn into angels. Her face

peeks around a scarlet poinsettia
on the hearth, floats in the bare spot
on the Christmas tree. The weight
of her absence hangs heavy,
bends the bough of the Douglas fir.

Traveling Companions

I take you with me, even to Central America-
Belize, land of the Maya-
they disappeared, left few clues.
Much like you, except
there was nobody to mourn them.

I carry you through the rain forest.
Gaze penetrates foliage as if wishes
could make a toucan appear,
or a stillborn baby's heart beat.
I explore the ruins, climb temple steps
until my legs ache, wonder
how an entire civilization ends.

We sail to the cays. Like a pelican
I dive again and again, float
buoyant over the barrier reef,
follow schools of parrot fish and tetras
as they dart among coral
like the flash of neon light sticks.
Palm trees survive by bending in acquiescence
to tropical gales; I whisper your name
in exotic locales.

Kokopelli's Promise

I am the colors of the southwest,
terracotta of the earth, turquoise of the sky,
the lavender and grape of shadowed canyon walls
where a flute melody hangs
one drawn-out note at a time
floating downward

to where I wait, alone by the river bed.
I am a spirit dancer
swaying to my own lullaby
in tandem with cottonwoods,
a Kokopelli calling for the babies
who are no longer of this world
to join me in celebration of the sunset.

As the moon rises from the canyon
to take its place in the nocturnal quilt,
I rock your babies to sleep
and lay them in their star cradles,
the multiverse their nursery,
meteor showers the kisses they blow back to earth.

Look up- you shall see them again

Things I Can't Remember

Weather on the day I was born, although
I don't know why that matters. The name
of the actor whose death was on the mid-day news.
The last time I went to church
for something other than a funeral.

What I meant to tell my brother
when I call Sunday afternoon. Instead,
we talk about a pub in London
whose name he can't recall. We'd met
his friend Steve there on my fiftieth birthday.

Whether I donated my black cashmere
sweater to a clothing drive. I spend a snowy
Sunday emptying dresser drawers, find
a silk blouse wrapped in tissue, and a suede
cowboy vest I bought my newborn grandson.

Where I hid Christmas presents I couldn't find
last year. If I've already read the paperback
I purchase in the airport. One hour into
an eight hour flight, realize I read and didn't like it.
The symbols on the remote for my home security alarm.

Which year I went to Santa Fe for Thanksgiving
with my parents and brother. I scroll
through digital photos on my computer,
search for the date stamp. 2006, the last
November my father was alive.

Love, Vincent

I start to delete the e-mail from Vincent, not knowing
anybody by that name, when I realize the address
is my father's. Last week he had surgery to remove
a squamous cell growth from his earlobe. As I read
his brief morning greeting, I again see his ear
swaddled like a miniature mummy, his hazel eyes
dulled with pain and fear. I type a quick reply,
better van Gogh than Picasso, and sign it
your sunflower.

A Phone Call after Midnight

never brings good news. My father's
bedside dialysis line has clotted again,
third night in a row, after his family
stumbled home from the hospital
to shed tears hidden not only from him,
but from each other.

The doctor says my father, intubated
and less responsive each day,
communicates in the only language
he can access, declares his wishes
to those who will listen.

I drink coffee until daybreak, drive
to my childhood home. Mum
sits on the patio, stares
at the overgrown clematis Dad planted,
shakes her head when I start
to speak. She puts on gardening gloves,
picks up the pruner, clips
until violet flowers spring free,
released from the confines
of tangled vine. Chooses a blossom
the shade of midnight for Dad,

a jolt of color against the white sheets
and metal of the ICU.
Dad died that evening,
his final exhale so gentle
it didn't ruffle the faded
flower resting on his chest.

Resurrection

The first Easter after Dad died
I waited for him to come back to life.
I sat at dinner, silence broken
by klink of fork against china,
swish and crackle of ice
as I stirred sugar into my tea.
I tried to ignore the whispered *hypocrite,*
you don't believe in the resurrection.

I am responsible for my father's
death. I'm the one who implored
the ICU doctors to convince my brother
it was time to forgo life-sustaining treatment,
to explain that our father now existed
in a realm we could not access.

First child, oldest daughter,
I'm the one who rested my head
on Dad's chest, strained to hear
his fading heartbeat, pressed my fingers
against the once-pulsing artery in his neck,
pushed the call button and told the nurse
his final exhale was at 5 p.m.

Elegy for Jim: A Love Song

College sweethearts, 1949:
a Marine who saw action
on Guadalcanal and a sheltered girl,
youngest of three daughters.
He pursued her,

DuPont wooed him.
They settled in Delaware,
raised three children,
buried the middle one
on a July day
so hot sweat obscured
their tears. Silent grief
shadowed them, swelled
to fill the emptiness.

Laughter of grandchildren,
then great-grandchildren,
soared to the top
of their living room's
cathedral ceiling, left
no room for melancholy.
He lit Hanukkah candles,
hid matzo at Passover.
Like a wizard, she cast
a spell of love with brisket
and chicken soup.

One Wednesday
he swam laps at the Y,
paid the electric bill,
shelled peas, fell ill

in the evening. Another
sweltering day,
June this time.
She sat motionless
as he was lowered
into the ground.
Fifty-eight years
of marriage reduced
to a few prayers,
some trowels of dirt

and forty lines of poetry.

Semper Fi

He never talked about his shrapnel wounds,
never bragged his battalion took that Pacific island.
Long after the autumn day I cut school
for the national moratorium, I learned
my father served on Guadalcanal.

I belted Country Joe and the Fish, hitchhiked to anti-war rallies.
My sister too stoned to protest even her curfew.
Brother, hair below his shoulders, didn't register
for the draft. Silent, Dad raised the flag
in our front yard every Veteran's Day.

Each August he dragged us to Houston,
Philadelphia, Las Vegas, 1st Marines
reunions. Legs encased in nylon, Mum
attended wives' teas. We smoked dope
in the bushes, ordered room service by the pool.

After he died I sorted his things, found a cigar box
full of ribbons, medals, threadbare campaign patches.
My thumb rubbed ridges of the blood–red
embroidered "1" the way I once traced
translucent scar tissue on his left hand.

Mt. Tibidabo

My brother and I ride with Mum,
seated backwards in the funicular,
to the top of Mt. Tibidabo, feel the chill
as we rise through the forest of pines.
Barcelona drops away
like a scene in an extended zoom lens.

We wander the amusement park
surrounding the Temple de Sagrat Cor,
pause before the giant foam dominoes
scattered across smooth cement.
If Dad were here,
he would be on his hands and knees
arranging them in a lightning bolt
pattern. I would ride the two-level
wooden carousel with him, perched
on the black horse, purple flowers
carved into its bridle. We would wave
to Mum each time we glided by.

After we three descend
I arrange a family photo, Mt. Tibidabo
in the background. My brother's hands
in his pockets, right foot extended
for a quick getaway. Mum stands alone
in the mist, hugs her jacket close,
stills her shiver. From the top
of the mountain, Jesus looks down
on us, arms spread wide,
like Icarus about to take flight.

Waldo Canyon Wildfire

Parched hills around Colorado Springs
feed the greedy fire. Whipped
by wind gusts, flames stampede
through mountain canyons like buffalo.
Smoke plumes swirl, obscure sections
of Pike's Peak, billow across I-25,
rain ash on rescue workers.
A fireman douses his head with water, winces
as he touches his singed eyebrows.
Hundreds of houses gone, charred car frames
all that remain.

Soot coats the cowboy motel
where I once soaked in an outdoor hot tub,
watched red rocks spotlighted by the summer moon.
I called Dad from a phone booth in Garden of the Gods,
one minute anywhere in the US, twenty-five cents.
Conversation cut off mid-sentence.

My father gone now too, five years
this month. His death as improbable
as cinder-covered columbines, tangerine
sky backlit from the setting sun,
midnight broken by the blazing outline
of homes glowing on the hillsides.

Sweet Baby James

Five years after Dad's death
I find a box with his birth announcement,
baby book, packet of photos.
For the first time I see my grandmother's
handwriting, loops and swirls
made by a woman I never knew,
the woman whose name I carry.

Family Reunion

I drive to Baltimore, bring a bag of seashells,
greet my younger sister first.
Walk along mulch paths, make my way
to the tree-line where my cousin's wife rests.
Stop to visit my uncle and favorite aunt,
my mother's older sister. Next
to them, my parents. I place shells, leave
holiday photos of sisters in aprons,
their husbands' grins wide as Montana,
arms slung across shoulders. The toddlers
in those pictures grandparents now,
two grandchildren at this reunion.

Gloaming

Early evening, after sunset melts
into the horizon, before the sky
gives way to the moon.
There is no shade to describe this time,
the heartbeat that marks the transition
from day to night, no named color for grief.

About the Author

Delaware native Nina Bennett is the author of *Sound Effects* (2013, Broadkill Press Key Poetry Series), and *Mix Tape* (2018). Her poetry has been nominated for the Best of the Net, and has appeared in numerous journals and anthologies. Awards include 2014 Northern Liberties Review Poetry Prize, and second-place in poetry book category from the Delaware Press Association (2014). A lifelong social activist, Nina is a healthcare provider with a subspecialty in secondary trauma and end-of-life issues. She is a founding member of the writing group TransCanal Writers. *(Five Bridges: A Literary Anthology)*.

www.transcanalwriters.org

www.ingramcontent.com/pod-product-compliance
Lightning Source LLC
LaVergne TN
LVHW091321080426
835510LV00007B/601